Contents

How to use this book

Speech bubbles raise interesting questions that you can discuss with others in your group.

Double or quits

Place value

A1

1, 2, 4, 8, …What happens if you keep on doubling? How many times must you double to reach a thousand? Ten thousand? One hundred thousand? One million?

1   This table shows some of the numbers you get when you keep doubling from 1. Copy and complete the table then see how much further you can go!

1	doubled is		2	doubled is	4
8	doubled is			doubled is	
64	doubled is			doubled is	
512	doubled is			doubled is	
4096	doubled is			doubled is	
32768	doubled is			doubled is	
262144	doubled is			doubled is	
2097152	doubled is			doubled is	
	doubled is			doubled is	
	doubled is			doubled is	

2   Write in words all of the numbers that appear in this doubling pattern between 1000 and 1000000.

Start with *one thousand and twenty four*.

End with *five hundred and twenty four thousand, two hundred and eighty eight*.

eXtra Investigate the pattern in the final digits of the numbers from the doubling table. It starts 1, 2, 4, 8, 6, 2, … How does it continue? Investigate other doubling patterns starting with numbers less than ten. What happens to the final digits?

③

If you finish the main activity before the end of the lesson, you can move on to the Extra activity.

Yellow boxes give you useful tips to help you understand the questions.

Double or quits

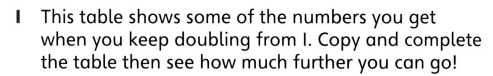

1, 2, 4, 8, …What happens if you keep on doubling? How many times must you double to reach a thousand? Ten thousand? One hundred thousand? One million?

1   This table shows some of the numbers you get when you keep doubling from 1. Copy and complete the table then see how much further you can go!

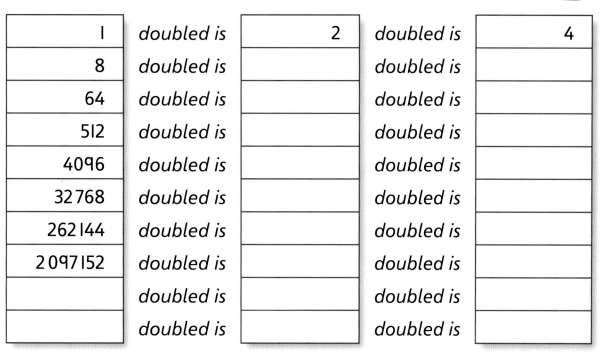

1	doubled is		2	doubled is		4
8	doubled is			doubled is		
64	doubled is			doubled is		
512	doubled is			doubled is		
4096	doubled is			doubled is		
32 768	doubled is			doubled is		
262 144	doubled is			doubled is		
2 097 152	doubled is			doubled is		
	doubled is			doubled is		
	doubled is			doubled is		

2   Write in words all of the numbers that appear in this doubling pattern between 1000 and 1 000 000.

Start with *one thousand and twenty-four*.

End with *five hundred and twenty-four thousand, two hundred and eighty-eight*.

Investigate the pattern in the final digits of the numbers from the doubling table. It starts 1, 2, 4, 8, 6, 2, … How does it continue? Investigate other doubling patterns starting with numbers less than ten. What happens to the final digits?

Roman numerals

Originally our numerals came from India. They were used by the Arabic peoples of the Middle East and then passed to Europe. We call them 'Arabic numerals'. Ancient Romans used a numeral system adapted from Etruscan numerals. Roman numerals are still used today.

Roman	I	V	X	L	C	D	M
Arabic	1	5	10	50	100	500	1000

Roman letters can be combined to make all numbers.

Roman	II	VIII	XI	LXV	CXX	DCL	MDI
Arabic	2	8	11	65	120	650	1501

Originally 4 was written as IIII but now we shorten it to IV (meaning I less than 5). In the same way VIIII is also IX.

1 Copy and complete this table using shortened Roman numbers.

Roman		XVII		LXIV		DCCVIII	
Arabic	7		29		145		3620

We get our word calculation from 'calculi' – small stones used on a Roman counting board.

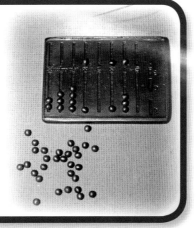

MMCMXXVII?

eXtra

How did the Romans write numbers from 4000 up to 1000000? Explore how addition and multiplication can be done with Roman numerals.

Find the number

A I am less than 3500.

B I am more than 3200.

C I am an odd number.

D My digits add to 12.

3081

3599   3398

3801

4008

1 Which of the statements are true for the numbers above?

Remember, more than one statement may be true for a number.

2 Make up four statements for these numbers.

Use what you know about numbers.

8750

8509

9058

9801

9913

3 Write which statements are true for each number.

4 Choose your own set of numbers and make up statements for them. Try them out on others in your group. Can they solve yours? Can you solve theirs?

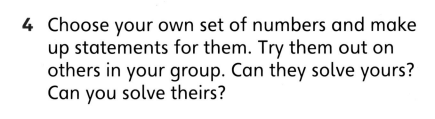

eX**tra** Choose four different digits, such as 1, 4, 5 and 9. Find all the different numbers that can be made with these four digits. Write out your numbers in order of size.

How can you make sure you have found all the numbers?

A1

Triple multiplying

1   What happens if you multiply these numbers together?

2   3   4

Now try with these multiplications.

2   4 × 2 × 4 =

3   2 × 5 × 2 =

4   5 × 3 × 1 =

Find the possible missing multipliers.

5   ☐ × ☐ × 4 = 40

6   ☐ × 3 × ☐ = 36

7   ☐ × ☐ × ☐ = 100

8   Choose any three digit cards and find their product. Show your working.
Write out the product (but not the multipliers). Swap with someone in
your group. Can you find the multipliers to make their product?

eXtra

What always happens to the product if …
*   **one of the three digits chosen is a 2?**
*   **one of the three digits chosen is a 5?**
*   **one is an even digit and another is a 5?**

Packing boxes

I 100 eggs are packed in boxes of 6. How many boxes are filled? How many eggs are left over?

2 What if 100 eggs were packed in boxes of 12?

How many boxes are used and how many eggs are left if these numbers of eggs are put in boxes of 6? What about boxes of 12?

3 65 eggs   **4** 80 eggs   **5** 119 eggs

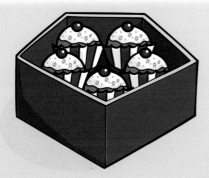 

Cupcakes are packed in red boxes of 5 and blue boxes of 8. You must put all the cupcakes into boxes.

> For 42 cupcakes the best solution is to use 2 red boxes (10 cupcakes) and 4 blue boxes (32 cupcakes).

Find the best way to pack these cupcakes with none left over.

6 60 cupcakes   **7** 81 cupcakes   **8** 100 cupcakes

> What are the best ways to pack boxes? Can you see any patterns?

 Try packing cereal bars into boxes of 7 and 11, using the above numbers. What is the largest number you cannot pack successfully?

Extending number pairs

Copy and complete these number pairs.

1 £554 + ☐ = £1000

2 £393 + ☐ = £1000

3 6600 + ☐ = 10 000

4 2100 + ☐ = 10 000

5 73 000 + ☐ = 100 000

6 86 200 + ☐ = 100 000

7 900 000 + ☐ = 1 000 000

8 480 000 + ☐ = 1 000 000

9 $3\frac{1}{2}$ + ☐ = 10

10 $6\frac{1}{2}$ + ☐ = 10

11 $7\frac{1}{4}$ + ☐ = 10

12 $9\frac{3}{4}$ + ☐ = 10

Solve these calculations.

148 + ☐ + 16 = 216

337 + ☐ + 29 = 529

730 + ☐ + 345 = 1345

681 + ☐ + 112 = 1112

What do you notice?

Word problems

Solve these word problems.

1 Nadia wants to find out what her baby weighs. She holds her baby and stands on the scales. The reading is 71 kg. Then she steps on the scales without her baby and the reading is 63 kg.

How much does the baby weigh?

2 Patrick needs to help the vet weigh his dog. He steps on the scales with the dog. The vet takes a reading of 122 kg. The vet takes the dog off the scales and asks Patrick to stay on. The reading is 88 kg.

How much does the dog weigh?

3 Lucy is making a batch of strawberry jam. She fills up some jam jars. Then she wonders how much jam there is in each jar. An empty jar weighs 186 g. A full jar of jam weighs 450 g.

In grams, how much jam is in each jar?

4 Emil is making chutney. His jars are all the same size. An empty jar with the lid on weighs 372 g. Emil weighs three full jars with the lids on. Jar A weighs 645 g, Jar B weighs 650 g and Jar C weighs 660 g.

In grams, how much chutney is there in each of the jars?

How much chutney is there in all three jars?

 Make up your own word problems like these. Ask other children in the class to try and solve them.

Investigating 2D shapes

How many new shapes can be made by fitting a triangle and a quadrilateral together?

1 How many different 2D shapes can you find?

I think there are four different shapes!

I think there are eight different shapes!

You're both right! What rules are you using?

2 If you found four shapes, do you understand how eight shapes can be found? Find the other four shapes.

If you found eight shapes, why do you think some people only find four shapes?

3 What is the rule for finding four shapes or eight shapes?

4 Why are there eight possible shapes and no more?

5 Did you find any triangles? How many?

6 Did you find any quadrilaterals? How many?

7 Did you find any pentagons? How many?

8 Did you find any hexagons? How many?

9 A triangle and a quadrilateral have seven sides in total. How can they be joined to make shapes with more or less sides?

There are four different angles in your triangle and quadrilateral.

10 Shade each equal angle a different colour. How do these angles combine to make the angles in your eight new shapes?

eXtra

With each of your new shapes you can make a tile pattern, called a tessellation, like this. Make eight copies of one of your shapes. Begin to make a tessellation. Investigate how it is possible to continue the pattern.

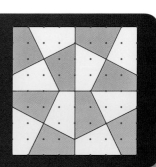

Rotational symmetry

> This shape does not have a line of symmetry, but a straight line can be drawn across it to make two halves that are exactly the same shape and size.
>
>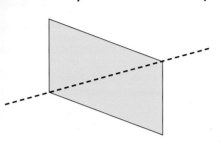

1 On PCM 4, draw another line that cuts this shape into two halves that are exactly the same. Mark the point where these two lines cross.

> This point is the **centre of rotational symmetry** of the shape. If you put your finger on this point and turn the page upside-down, the shape looks just the same.
>
> So the shape has **rotational symmetry**.

2 Investigate if the five shapes on PCM 4 have rotational symmetry. Do this by halving them with straight lines again.

3 One of these shapes is the odd one out. It has not quite got rotational symmetry. Which one is it?

a  b  c  d

extra **Use dotted paper to make up your own rotational symmetry patterns.**

2D shape patterns

Look at this crazy paving of triangles. Can you see any **scalene** triangles? Any **isosceles** triangles? Any **equilateral** triangles?

1 Complete the table on PCM 5 with the properties of the three scalene triangles. Use the words in the oval to help you. The first one is completed for you.

2 Look at the other triangles in the crazy paving. Complete the tables on PCM 5 to describe these four triangles. Use the words in the oval to help you.

3 Look at this crazy paving of quadrilaterals.

Describe the differences between these shapes looking at any equal sides, equal angles and special angles such as right angles.

Use the words in the oval on PCM 5 to help you.

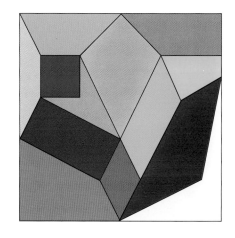

 e**X**tra **Pick a quadrilateral. A partner can ask you questions to guess your chosen shape. Think about equal sides, equal angles, and special angles such as right angles.**

Imperial units

In the Imperial system of units, lengths are measured in inches, feet, yards and miles, instead of millimetres, centimetres, metres and kilometres.

5 centimetres is about 2 inches.

8 kilometres is about 5 miles.

Use this information to solve these problems.

1 How many centimetres are there in 12 inches (1 foot)?

2 How many centimetres are there in 3 feet (1 yard)?

3 How many inches are there in a metre?

4 How many kilometres are there in 20 miles?

5 How many kilometres are there in 100 miles?

6 How many miles are there in 120 kilometres?

7 We can set out this kind of problem using a grid. Use your answers to copy and complete this grid.

Mudvillage 20 miles

centimetres	5	
inches	2	12

kilometres	8	
miles	5	20

8 Make up some of your own problems, using different units.

4 litres is about 7 pints

9 litres is about 2 gallons (16 pints)

30 grams is about 1 ounce

11 pounds is about 5 kilograms

e**X**tra Use the internet or reference books to find some exact conversion amounts (for example, 1 inch is exactly 2·54 cm). Use a calculator to check how close your approximate answers were for questions 1 to 6.

Pairs of tetrominoes

A **tetromino** is four identical squares joined edge to edge.

What are the areas of these tetrominoes?

Here are the five tetrominoes.

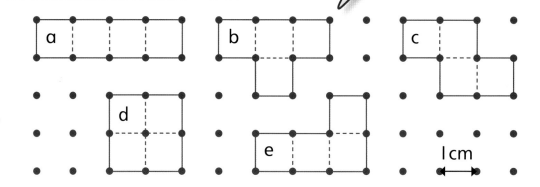

1 cm

We can 'walk' around each shape, taking one 'step' between each dot. Walk around Tetromino a: 4 steps, turn, 1 step, turn, 4 steps, turn, 1 step. This is a total of 10 steps. **The perimeter is 10 cm.**

1 How many steps do you need to walk around each tetromino? Record the perimeters.

What do you notice?

Fit any two tetrominoes together and draw the new shape on dotted paper. Investigate the new shape's perimeter and area.

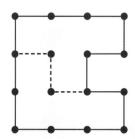

Perimeter = 14 cm

Area = 8 cm²

2 What is the maximum and minimum perimeter you can find? Show your workings.

eXtra

Fit all five tetrominoes together to make a single shape. What is the area and perimeter? Compare your shape with the shapes of others in your group. Can you make a shape which has the shortest possible perimeter? The longest possible perimeter?

Areas of rectangles

Can you see patterns in the areas of rectangles and squares?

Some rectangles, like these ones, have a difference of one unit between the side lengths.

Their areas are 'oblong numbers', like 2 or 12.

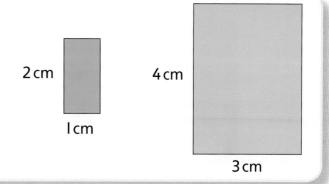

1 Explore patterns in the areas of this type of rectangle. Can you predict the area of the next rectangle? And the next?

Some rectangles, like these ones, are squares and have all sides the same length.

Their areas are 'square numbers', like 4 or 9.

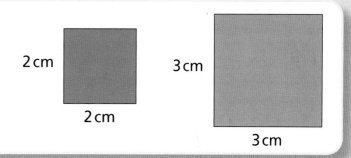

2 Explore patterns in the areas of squares.

3 Explore rectangles which have one pair of sides two units longer than the other pair of sides. Start with 1 by 3, then 2 by 4, 3 by 5, and so on.

4 Compare your pattern for this set of rectangles with your pattern for squares. Is there a connection? What do you notice?

eXtra Cut out the sets of rectangles from PCM 6. Starting with the largest one, place the rectangles on top of one another, lining up the top left corner. Look at the L-shaped pieces of each rectangle that are left uncovered. What are the areas of these pieces? Can you see a pattern?

All sorts of bears

There are lots of different bears in the world. How can we tell which one is which?

PCM 8 has some cards with information about these bears.

1 Read the cards and use the internet or a book about bears to find out more facts. Add any new facts to your cards.

2 Work as a group to think of eight questions to ask to work out which bear is which. The questions must have *Yes* or *No* answers.

3 Take it in turns to choose a bear. Keep it secret! The rest of the group ask the eight questions and guess which bear it is.

Spectacled bear

Is it dangerous?

Does it live in the wild in South America?

Does it eat honey?

Is it black?

  Find out the heights and weights of the bears. Put them in size order. Which bears are taller than the door? Are any bears your height? Shorter than you?

Make your own pictograms

Class 4 did a survey to find out what was the most popular type of puzzle in the class. Here are their results.

Crosswords	Jigsaws	Codewords	Wordsearches	Sudoku
6	7	4	8	5

1 Use this data to make a frequency table.

2 Now make a pictogram to represent this data. Remember to include a key to explain how many people each symbol represents!

> What symbol would you like to use? How many people should each symbol represent?

3 Here is a table of the favourite puzzles chosen by a large sample of people. Draw a pictogram for this data. Choose a suitable number of people for each symbol to represent.

Crosswords	Jigsaws	Codewords	Wordsearches	Sudoku
40	18	14	4	24

4 Compare the two sets of data. Do the pictograms make it easier to compare the two sets?

eXtra There are simple programs on the internet that let you put in your own data, and make pictograms using different symbols and meanings for each symbol. Try some programs out with this data.

Hexadria

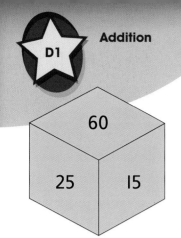

In this hexagon the numbers in the rhombus shapes are all multiples of five.

They add to 100.

1   On PCM 9, find other ways of making 100 using three different multiples of 5.

> How many can you find?

Imagine the hexagon is a cube.

The rule for each cube is that opposite faces total 100.

> The numbers on the opposite faces of this cube are 40, 75 and 85.

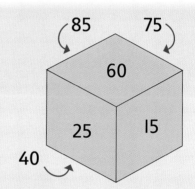

2   What are the numbers on the opposite faces of your cubes?

3   What is the total of the three hidden faces of your cubes? Why?

Hexadria are made by overlapping six hexagons to make a larger hexagon. The numbers on the three rhombuses of each small hexagon must add to the same total.

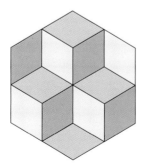

4   Try to complete a hexadrian using multiples of 5 up to 95 to make a total of 100 in each small hexagon.

5   What totals do the six centre numbers make?

 Try to find the hexadria with the smallest possible total for each hexagon. What about the largest possible total? You can use whole numbers only (but not 0) and all 12 numbers must be different.

Adding consecutive numbers

Adding two consecutive numbers

1 Explore what happens when you add two consecutive numbers. Describe any patterns that you find.

Example:
5 + 6 = 11

Adding three consecutive numbers

2 Explore what happens when you add three consecutive numbers. Describe any patterns that you find.

Example:
7 + 8 + 9 = 24

Adding more than three consecutive numbers

3 Investigate adding larger sets of consecutive numbers. Describe any patterns that you find.

Examples:
4 + 5 + 6 + 7 = 22
12 + 13 + 14 + 15 + 16 = 70
6 + 7 + 8 + 9 + 10 + 11 = 51

4 Try to write a rule for the total of any set of four consecutive numbers.

5 Try to write rules for the totals of other size sets.

Making totals in different ways

> The smallest total that can be made in two different ways is 9.
> 4 + 5 and 2 + 3 + 4

6 What is the smallest total that can be made in three different ways? Four different ways?

eXtra It is not possible to make 8 by adding consecutive numbers. Is this true? Which other numbers can never be made by adding consecutive numbers? Is there a pattern to these numbers?

Before and after the hour

Use the linking cards from PCM II. Sort them into their sets A, B, C and D.

Cards follow on from one card to the next, like this:

9:45 A

30 minutes later

leads on to

10:15 A

35 minutes earlier

because 10:15 is 30 minutes after 9:45.

10:15 is then the starting point for the next link in the set of cards. What time is 35 minutes earlier than 10:15? The answer to that question will be on the next card in the loop.

I Practise making a chain with one set of cards. Repeat for another set of cards.

2 Play the linking card game.

Rules
- Shuffle all 24 cards together.
- Deal them out between your group.
- Any player who has a 9:45 card may start the game.
- Take turns to see who can follow the last card played.
- Keep checking that all cards played are correct.
- The first player to use up all their cards wins the game.

£4000

3 Play the game again. See if you can play it faster than before.

4 Play again but this time do not take turns. Play your cards as soon as you can go!

eXtra

12:00   9:29   11:02   9:58   10:31   11:28

Design a chain of six cards that uses these six times of day, in any order. Swap your set with a partner. Solve your partner's chain.

Fractions of 60

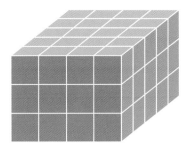

> There are 60 minutes in an hour. How many minutes are there in half an hour? How many minutes are there in other fractions of an hour?

1 Pair up these fractions of an hour with the correct numbers of minutes. Write out all the pairs.

> Some of the fractions and numbers will not pair up.

$\frac{1}{2}$ $\frac{1}{3}$ $\frac{2}{3}$ $\frac{1}{4}$ $\frac{3}{4}$ $\frac{1}{5}$ $\frac{3}{5}$ $\frac{1}{6}$ $\frac{1}{10}$ $\frac{5}{12}$ $\frac{1}{20}$

12   5   40   6   15   18   10   20   25   30   3

2 What are the numbers of minutes for the fractions that do not pair up?

3 What are the fractions for the numbers of minutes that do not pair up?

> Can you find any other fractions of an hour?

 eXtra $\frac{1}{2}$ of half an hour is 15 minutes. How many minutes do the fractions represent for half an hour? Two hours? Make up some questions about these amounts of time as fractions. Share these with the group.

Time zones

Times vary around the world because the Earth spins. Before time zones were set, the time could even vary as people travelled around Britain! This was difficult for the railways, and the very first time zone in the world was set up by British railway companies in 1847.

By 1929, most big countries had hourly time zones. Today, all nations use time zones. China uses a single time zone even though their country spreads across 5 hours of standard time lines of longitude. Australia has three different time zones so the east and west of the country are 2 hours different.

The International Date Line is not straight. It is drawn mostly straight, running through the Pacific Ocean, but it bends around groups of islands and the far eastern tip of Asia.

Each hour is a separate time zone. A day is 24 hours. There are 360 degrees of longitude around the Earth.

1　How many degrees wide is a standard time zone?

2　Plot the journey from PCM 12 on the world time zones map on PCM 13.

3　What happens to your body clock if you go around the world travelling east?

4　Imagine a journey of your own around the world travelling west. Use an atlas or the internet and the world time zones map to copy and complete the table on PCM 12.

eXtra **Find out more about Greenwich Mean Time, standard times and lines of longitude on the internet.**

Patterns in multiples

The twentieth-century English mathematician, G.H. Hardy, said that a *mathematician is a maker of patterns*. Hardy was very interested in an area of mathematics called 'number theory'. Number theory is the study of the properties of whole numbers. Patterns in number theory have been developed and studied for centuries.

G.H. Hardy

Here is the pattern for doubling.

This pattern only looks at the final digit. For example the arrow from **6** to **2** stands for **6** doubled is 1**2**; 1**6** doubled is 3**2**, and so on.

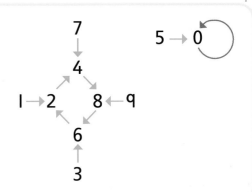

I Investigate the pattern for multiplying by 4 and draw a diagram to show it.

2 Draw a diagram to show the pattern for multiplying by 8.

> Can you see connections between your multiplication patterns and the doubling pattern?

Work out patterns for multiplying by these numbers.

3 multiplying by I   **4** multiplying by 5   **5** multiplying by 3

6 multiplying by 6   **7** multiplying by 7   **8** multiplying by 9

When they make patterns, mathematicians see what else they can find out and what new questions they can ask. For example, what do you notice about the numbers at the centre of your multiplication patterns? What other new questions can you ask?

23

Rainbow patterns

Can you see patterns of products in a multiplication square?

1	2	3	4	5	6	7	8	9	10
2	4	6	8	10	12	14	16	18	20
3	6	9	12	15	18	21	24	27	30
4	8	12	16	20	24	28	32	36	40
5	10	15	20	25	30	35	40	45	50
6	12	18	24	30	36	42	48	54	60
7	14	21	28	35	42	49	56	63	70
8	16	24	32	40	48	56	64	72	80
9	18	27	36	45	54	63	72	81	90
10	20	30	40	50	60	70	80	90	100

This is a pattern for the products of 20 in a multiplication square. The 20s make a curved pattern a bit like a rainbow.

Each 20 comes from a multiplication. We can record the multiplications in a list like this.

20
10 × 2
5 × 4
4 × 5
2 × 10

1 Copy this pattern onto the multiplication square on PCM 15.

2 Find other products that appear five or more times on the multiplication square. Use a different colour for each product.

3 Record the multiplications for each product in a list.

4 Imagine that your multiplication grid continued beyond 20. The product 20 would not appear again, but some of your other products would. Work out what other multiplications would give you the same products and add those to your product lists.

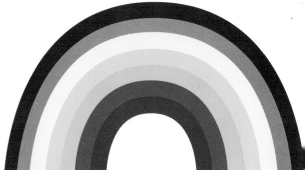

eXtra Which of the product numbers you have found have an odd number of multiplications in your table? Can you explain why?

Doubling and halving with fractions

Start with a multiplication fact. $6 \times 4 = 24$

Halve the first number and double the second. The product stays the same. $3 \times 8 = 24$

Try repeating the process a few times. $1\frac{1}{2} \times 16 = 24$

Check that each line still gives the same product. $\frac{3}{4} \times 32 = 24$

> For $\frac{3}{4} \times 32$ you can say *three quarters of thirty-two*.

1 Here are some multiplications. Copy and complete the tables. Extend each table by two rows. What is the answer to each calculation?

10×3	18×5	14×6
$5 \times$	$\times$	$\times 12$
$\times$	$\times$	$\times$
$1\frac{1}{4} \times$	$\times 40$	$\times$

2 Make up three multiplications of your own. You might end up with some tricky looking multiplications but you will be able to find the answers!

3 Try it backwards. Double the first number and halve the second one. Copy and complete these tables. Extend each table until you have two whole numbers.

$4 \times$	$\times$	$\times$
$\times$	$\times$	$\times$
$16 \times 3\frac{1}{4}$	$28 \times 2\frac{3}{4}$	$20 \times 3\frac{1}{4}$

Explore multiplying by 3 and dividing by 3.
Write a multiplication of two numbers, for example 2 × 4.
Multiply one number by 3 and divide the other by 3. What do you notice? Look at multiplying and dividing by 5.

Fraction games

The grubs

$1\frac{1}{2}$ $\frac{7}{8}$ $1\frac{3}{10}$ $\frac{3}{4}$ $1\frac{1}{3}$ $1\frac{1}{4}$ $\frac{5}{6}$ $\frac{1}{2}$

The frogs

$8\frac{7}{8}$ $9\frac{1}{5}$ $9\frac{1}{4}$ $8\frac{3}{5}$ $9\frac{7}{10}$ $8\frac{5}{6}$ $9\frac{3}{8}$ $9\frac{7}{12}$

The pool

$10\frac{1}{5}$ $10\frac{1}{3}$ $10\frac{1}{4}$ $10\frac{1}{8}$ $10\frac{1}{6}$ $10\frac{1}{2}$ $10\frac{1}{10}$ $10\frac{1}{12}$

1 Add each grub number to a frog number to make a pool number.
Can you match up all the numbers?

Here is a second pool
of numbers.

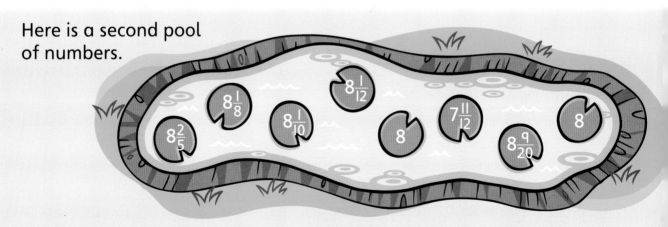

$8\frac{2}{5}$ $8\frac{1}{8}$ $8\frac{1}{10}$ $8\frac{1}{12}$ 8 $7\frac{11}{12}$ $8\frac{9}{20}$ 8

2 Subtract each grub number from a frog number to make a number in
the second pool.

eXtra **Design your own grub, frog and pool
numbers to work like these.**

Investigating fraction sentences

On PCM 16 are some regular polygons and stars called polygrams.

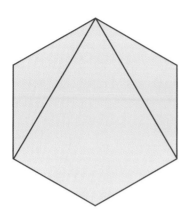

Here is a regular hexagon, with two of its diagonals drawn on.
These diagonals do not cross.
They form three new shapes.

> What fraction of the hexagon is each part?

The fraction sentence for this hexagon is
$\frac{2}{3} + \frac{1}{6} + \frac{1}{6} = 1$

1 Explore what other sets of fractions of the hexagon you can make. Use one, two or three diagonals. Record your findings in fraction sentences.

2 Investigate with other polygons or polygrams as your starting shape.

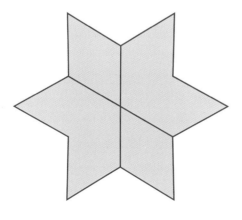

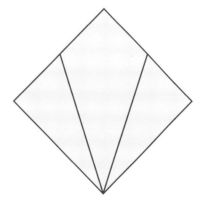

eXtra

In maths, stars are called polygrams. They are made from a pattern of diagonals in a regular polygon. Here is an example with an octagon. What different polygrams can you find?

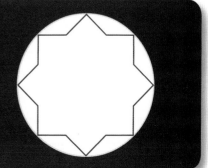

Larger numbers

 add 100

 subtract 1000

add 10 000

add 1000

subtract 10 000

subtract 100

1 Choose a 5-digit number. Throw a dice once, then add or subtract to match the dice throw.

For example

41 461 − 100 = 41 361

2 Work with a partner. Throw two dice and use both the codes. Throw two dice again and repeat this for all nine numbers.

For example

50 064 + 100 = 50 164

50 164 + 1000 = 51 164

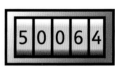

3 Try with three dice!

4 Now make up your own code or use one of these. Again use one, two and then three dice and try to repeat for all nine numbers.

Set B	Set C	Set D
1 add 200	1 add 500	1 add 90
2 subtract 200	2 subtract 500	2 subtract 90
3 add 2000	3 add 5000	3 add 900
4 subtract 2000	4 subtract 5000	4 subtract 900
5 add 20 000	5 add 50 000	5 add 9000
6 subtract 20 000	6 subtract 50 000	6 subtract 9000

Secretly write two 5-digit numbers. Choose a dice code and tell it to your partner. Your partner throws a dice. Use your code to add to or subtract from your numbers. Tell your partner your results. Can your partner work out your secret numbers? Now try with two dice. Three dice.

Adding sequences with Gauss

Carl Friedrich Gauss was born in Germany and started primary school when he was seven. His mathematical ability was noticed almost immediately. His teachers were amazed when Gauss was asked to add up all of the numbers from 1 to 100. They had given him this task as they thought the many additions would keep him busy for a long while. However, Carl thought he had found a quick way to calculate it and almost immediately answered 5050.

1 Try adding the numbers from 1 to 100. Was Carl Gauss correct?

What strategies did you use? Did others in your group use the same ones? Can you work out how Carl Gauss did it?

Here are some other questions about adding consecutive numbers.

2 Add all the consecutive whole numbers from 10 to 19.

3 Add all the consecutive whole numbers from ⁻100 to 100.

4 Add all the consecutive odd numbers from 1 to 19.

5 Add all the consecutive odd numbers from 21 to 39.

6 Add all the consecutive even numbers from 10 to 30.

This time you are told the sum but you need to find out which consecutive numbers were added.

7 Seven consecutive numbers totalling 84.

8 Five consecutive odd numbers totalling 75.

9 Three consecutive even numbers totalling 96.

 Invent and share your own consecutive number problems. Use different patterns of numbers but always have the same gap between each one, for example add 17, 22, 27, 32, 37, 42 and 47.

Estimating game

These children are playing an estimating game. They don't do the calculation, they just estimate the answer. If they correctly estimate that the answer is between two numbers, then they stay in the game. The winner is the player whose estimate has the smallest difference.

Calculation: 23 × 17		Estimates			
Name(s)	**Between**		**Difference**	**In/Out**	**Rank**
Anil	350	400	50	IN	3rd
Betty	400	420	20	OUT	
Chris	380	400	20	IN	2nd
Dipak	385	395	10	IN	1st
The answer is: 391					

Betty is out because the answer does not come within her estimate.

Play the game with your group, using the score sheets on PCM 17.

Choose someone to be the game-master. The game-master chooses the calculation and times the estimating. They find the right answer with a calculator and check everyone's estimates. Then they score the estimates, and decide who wins.

The game-master chooses from these calculations.

33 × 27 $\frac{1}{5}$ of 2475 $\frac{4}{5}$ of 950   15 × £7·45

Play the game several times, taking turns to be the game-master.

eXtra Play the estimating game again, but this time invent some really tricky multiplications and divisions when it is your turn as the game-master.

Exploring arithmagons

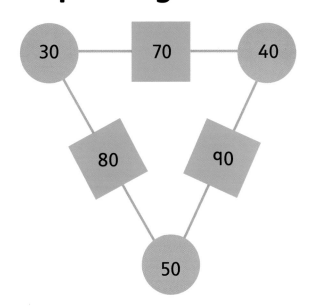

In an arithmagon the circle numbers on each line add to give the number in the square between them.

This is a triangle arithmagon.

We can put different multiples of 10 in the circles and work out the numbers in the squares.

Are there any patterns?

1   Complete the first four arithmagons on PCM 19.

2   In triangle arithmagons, if you are given one circle number and two square numbers next to it, how do you find the number in the last square? Is there a pattern that could lead to a rule?

3   In triangle arithmagons, if you are given all the square numbers, how do you find the circle numbers? Can you find a rule? Does it work for square arithmagons?

4   Invent some problems using triangle and square arithmagons. You could even try using pentagon or hexagon arithmagons!

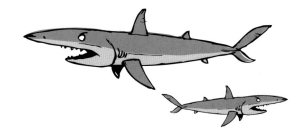

eXtra   **Explore what happens when you use a different rule for the arithmagon. For example, each square number is found by multiplying the numbers in the circles next to it. If the square numbers in a triangle arithmagon are 72, 54 and 12, what are the numbers in the circles? Now try making up your own rule. Write some problems for your partner to solve.**

Positive and negative number loops

Use the number line to answer the questions.

Adding 10 means going forward 10 on the line, and subtracting 10 means going back 10 along the line.

-50 -40 -30 -20 -10 0 10 20 30 40 50

1 Start at ⁻40. Add 60. What number do you reach?

2 Start at ⁺25. Subtract 40. What number do you reach?

3 Practise adding and subtracting from different start numbers.

Playing the game

- Together check that each set of linking cards from PCM 20 follows on to make a complete loop.
- Shuffle all 24 cards then deal them out between your group.
- Any player with a card with top left number **0** may start the game.
- Take turns to see if you have a card to follow the last card played.
- Check that each card played is the right answer. You can use the number line to check.
- The first player to use up all their cards wins the game.

Play the game again. Can you play it faster?
If you have time, try it without taking turns:
play your cards as soon as you can go!

eXtra

Here are four sets of six numbers. They are the answers from a set of linking cards. Each choose a different set. Use your numbers, in any order, to produce six mini-loop cards.

0	⁻75
⁺75	⁺50
⁻50	⁺25

0	⁺25
⁻50	⁺50
⁺75	⁻75

0	⁻45
⁺35	⁺25
⁻25	⁺65

0	⁺65
⁻25	⁺25
⁺35	⁻45

Halving and doubling shapes

1 Cut out the square on PCM 21. Find its centre and draw a straight line through the centre. Cut along this line and compare the two pieces you have made. What new shapes can be made with these pieces?

> Find the centre where the diagonals cross.

> To cut a shape in half you must go through the centre of the shape.

2 Explore halving and doubling shapes like this with the rectangle, the rhombus and the parallelogram on PCM 21. What do you find?

3 Draw one of the shapes from PCM 21 onto square dotted paper. Find the centre of the shape and draw a halving line. Draw a new shape you can make by doubling the two halves.

Keep halving and doubling the shapes until you get back to the shape you started with.

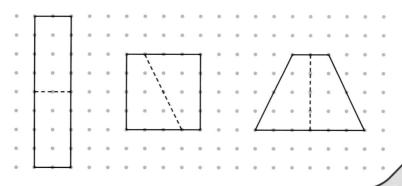

> Did you use the symmetry of the shapes to help you?

eXtra

**Here is an example where four small shapes can be put together to make a larger version of the same shape. This is quadrupling.
Explore quadrupling some shapes – do they always make a larger version of the same shape?**

Doubling chains

Look at this doubling chain for the number 1.

The number 1 has been doubled until it reaches a number over 100 000. This is a 6-digit number.

1   Start a chain for each of the numbers 1 to 9. Write the first four numbers in each chain. Then cross out any numbers that appear in another doubling chain.

What do you notice about the numbers you have left?

Doubling game

- Shuffle a set of digit cards 1–9.

- Place them face down.

- Each take a card. Keep it secret!

- Record the doubling chain for your digit card until you reach a 6-digit number. Check your doubling with a calculator.

- Write down the 6-digit number that you got to.

- Swap numbers with a partner.

- Try to work out, without a calculator, which digit card they started with.

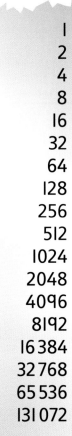

1
2
4
8
16
32
64
128
256
512
1024
2048
4096
8192
16384
32768
65536
131072

eXtra These 2-digit numbers have been doubled to 6-digit numbers. Which numbers do not match? What is the correct 6-digit number?

11	13	139264	168406
17	19	118784	106496
23	29	180224	155648

Steps to triangular numbers

Here are some sets of steps made from linking cubes.

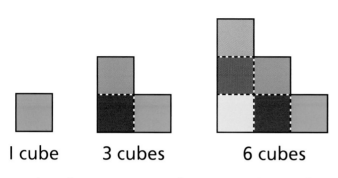

I cube   3 cubes   6 cubes

> Can you see a pattern in the number of cubes used to make each set of steps?

1 Make the next set of steps using cubes. Draw this set on square dotted paper. How many cubes did you use?

> These steps make a sequence called triangular numbers.

> Why might they be called triangular numbers?

2 Continue drawing the sets of steps until you reach a set that uses more than 100 cubes.

3 Colour in the number of cubes for each set on a 100-square.

4 Write the sequence in a line and write underneath it how many cubes are added with each new step.

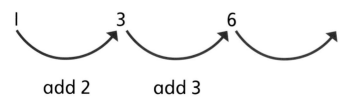

add 2   add 3

> What pattern can you see?

 eXtra Add together the first two triangular numbers. Now try adding the next two triangular numbers. What is special about the numbers you get? Is this the same for all pairs of triangular numbers?

Properties of polyhedra

 triangular prism   square pyramid 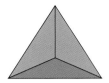 regular tetrahedron

This table shows what polygons are used to make polyhedra.

	Triangles	Squares
Triangular prism	2	3
Square pyramid	4	1
Regular tetrahedron	4	0

We can see that this triangular prism is made of three squares and two equilateral triangles.

1 Look at PCM 23. Use polygons to work out the number of vertices, edges and faces for each prism and pyramid. Use this information to complete the two tables.

What patterns can you see?

2 Work together to complete the table on PCM 24.

What patterns can you see?

eXtra **Use the internet to find out about deltahedra, antiprisms and dipyramids.**

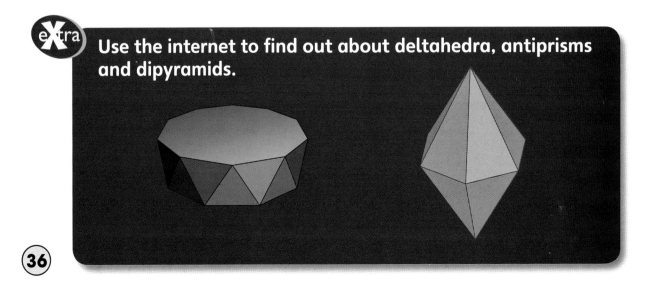

Pentominoes and cube nets

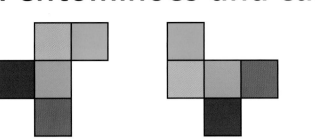 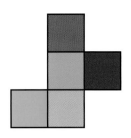 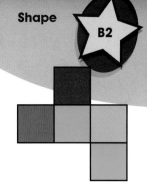

Pentominoes are made from five squares. These pictures show the same pentomino in four different positions. It can be rotated, flipped over or reflected but it only counts as one pentomino.

> What other ways can this pentomino be drawn?

I Draw all the pentominoes on square dot grid paper.
   How many are there?

> How did you make sure you found them all?

Some pentominoes can be folded to make an open cube.

2 Which pentominoes do you think will make open cubes?

3 Check whether you are right by cutting out the pentominoes and folding them up.

Some pentominoes can be made into closed cube nets when one more square is added.

4 Where should the sixth square be added to each of your open cube nets to make a closed cube net?

5 How many closed cube nets are there in total? Record them.

 What symmetries do your closed cube nets have?

Capacity puzzles

- Filling a bottle is one step.
- Pouring from one bottle to another is one step.
- Emptying a bottle is one step.

Write down the steps you need to get the target.

	Bottle 1	Bottle 2	Target
1	1·5 litres	4 litres	1 litre
2	1·5 litres	2·5 litres	2 litres
3	2 litres	2·5 litres	1 litre
4	2 litres	4·5 litres	5 litres

How many steps are you taking? Do you have a strategy?

Write down the steps you need to reach the target with three bottles.

	Bottle sizes			Target
5	75 cl	1·25 l	2 l	End up with two bottles containing 1 litre.
6	1·5 l	2 l	3·5 l	Start with the 3·5 litre bottle full of water. End with two bottles having 1 litre and one bottle having 1·5 litres.

eXtra

Make these capacity cards. Pick three cards to be your bottles.

25 cl	50 cl	75 cl	1 l	1·25 l
1·5 l	1·75 l	2 l	2·25 l	2·5 l

Place the rest of the cards face down. Take turns to turn over a card. Can you make that capacity using your bottles? If you can, keep that card. Repeat until there are no cards left. The winner has the most cards.

Nomograms

Nomograms were invented by two French mathematicians in 1889. The simplest nomograms are two scales on opposite sides of a line.

Nomograms are used for changing numbers between scales. For example, changing temperatures between Fahrenheit and Celsius, like on this thermometer.

A nomogram can also be a pair of lines that are drawn next to each other. They are given a scale and a special starting point.

Look at the litres and pints nomagram on PCM 25. Can you see how it works?

1 How many pints is 40 litres?

2 How many litres is 10 pints?

Nomograms can also be used for addition and subtraction.

The addition nomogram on PCM 25 shows a line drawn from 45 to 20, passing through 65.

The line shows that:

$45 + 20 = 65$ $20 + 45 = 65$ $65 - 20 = 45$ $65 - 45 = 20$

Draw lines on the addition nomogram to answer these calculations.

3 $10 + 45$ **4** $40 + 50$ **5** $80 - 30$ **6** $20 - 5$

Make your own addition nomogram using the blank scales on PCM 25. Decide what you add using your nomogram. It could be for adding money, whole numbers and tenths, fractions or lengths. Can you think of anything else you could add with your nomogram?

Timetables

PCM 26 shows part of a train timetable between London and Arundel.

1 How much earlier than 09:00 do Trains 1 to 4 arrive at Arundel?
How much later than 09:00 does Train 5 arrive at Arundel?

2 How long do people on Trains 3 and 5 spend at Three Bridges?

3 Work out total times for each journey from London to Arundel.

4 Which train journey takes the shortest time?

5 All the trains are being delayed by up to half an hour.
What is the latest train to leave London that can still arrive in Arundel before 09:00?

Look at the routes and flight times for *FlyTee* on PCM 26.

Jarek lives 25 minutes from Birmingham airport.
He flies to Belfast for lunch. The restaurant is
30 minutes from the airport and lunch starts at 13:00.
Jarek has to fly back to Birmingham that day.

6 Which two flights could Jarek take to Belfast?

7 Choose Jarek's flights and work out a good timetable for his day.

Rosa lives in Newcastle. She wants
to visit as many cities as she can in
one week.

Don't forget to get
Rosa home again!

8 Plan a timetable for Rosa for the week.

9 How long does Rosa spend flying, including
time spent at check-in and baggage collection?

e**X**tra

How can you get from Stansted to Belfast? Which flights do you recommend? Think about how much time is spent flying and the wait between flights. Plan some more two-stage journeys.

Side lengths and perimeters

> How does side length affect the perimeter of a quadrilateral?

A rectangle has a perimeter of 30 cm. What lengths could its sides be? Explore different side lengths in whole and half centimetres.

> It could be a square with sides of 7·5 cm.

Draw your rectangles on square dot paper. Find the areas.
For some rectangles, work out the areas without drawing them.

1 Which rectangle has the largest area? What is the area?

2 Which rectangle has an area nearest to 20 cm²?

3 Which rectangle has the smallest area? What is the area?

4 Draw a rectangle with a perimeter of 30 cm on square dot paper. Find the area.

Investigate ways to change the shape, but keep the perimeter at 30 cm.

For each new shape you draw, work out the area.

Area: 36 cm²

Area: 35 cm²

Area: 34 cm²

How many different areas can be made from your starting shape? Compare your results with the group.

> What do you notice?

 e**X**tra

Draw some quadrilaterals, with perimeters of 30 cm, on triangle dot paper. Only use whole centimetres for the side lengths. Find the areas by counting the triangles. Do you notice anything interesting?

Graphs and collecting data

People usually collect data to find the answer to a question.

> What are some questions that can be answered by collecting data?

PCM 28 has data collected by some children to answer a question. You do not know what the question is.

1 Put all the data from PCM 28 into a table.

> What question do you think the children are trying to answer?

2 What types of chart or graph could you use to show the data?
Choose a type of chart or graph.
What are the labels and titles you will use?
Will you need axes? What will your axes represent?
Use the data to draw your chart or graph.

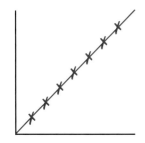
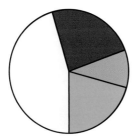
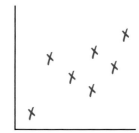
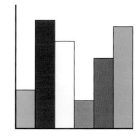

3 What might the data be showing? Can you see this in your table?
Can you see it in the graph or chart?

4 Compare your graph or chart with others. Do they show the same things? Are some graphs and charts easier to understand?

5 What is the answer to the question you think the children were asking?

 eXtra Write some questions you could collect data for.
How could you find the answer to one of your questions?
Make a survey or questionnaire to answer your question.
Could you collect the data differently?

Number targets

Anji chooses six digit cards: 0, 2, 3, 6, 7 and 9.
She uses them to make three additions.

6 3 7 + 2 0 9 = 846

7 9 0 + 2 3 6 = 1026

3 9 + 7 0 + 6 2 = 171

> Could you work out Anji's digit cards by looking at her totals? Could she get closer to 1000?

Anji and her friends make some new additions. The cards they use are shown next to their totals. What additions do they make?

1 Anji made totals of 1836, 1017 and 198.   2 4 6 7 8 9

2 Ben made totals of 1231, 1006 and 160.   0 2 4 5 6 8

3 Raul made totals of 1000, 505 and 100.   1 3 4 5 7 8

4 Jeni made totals of 1502, 1205 and 206.   0 5 6 7 8 9

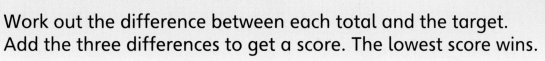

Play this game as a group.
Make three additions with the cards 0, 2, 4, 6, 7 and 9. Aim for these targets. Write down your additions and the totals.

- Target 1: Add two 3-digit numbers.
  Get as close to 1000 as you can.

- Target 2: Add two 3-digit numbers.
  Get as close to 900 as you can.

- Target 3: Add three 2-digit numbers.
  Get as close to 180 as you can.

Work out the difference between each total and the target.
Add the three differences to get a score. The lowest score wins.

Which six cards could you choose to give the lowest possible difference between two 3-digit numbers?

Palindromes

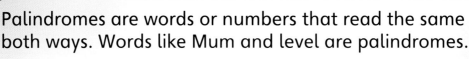

4994

121

Don't nod

926629

Racecar

Mum

Too bad — I hid a boot   **82 528**   Was it a cat I saw

> Palindromes are words or numbers that read the same both ways. Words like Mum and level are palindromes.
>
> ## Never odd or even

1   Find the palindromes in the number square on PCM 29. Colour them in one colour. What times-table are they in?

You can make palindromes using these steps.

A   Choose a number from the PCM.   **37**

B   Reverse the number.   **37 + 73 = 110**
    Add the two together.

C   Is it a palindrome?   **110 is not a palindrome**

D   Repeat steps B and C until   **110 + 011 = 121**
    you get a palindrome.

2   • Share out the numbers on the PCM that are not palindromes.

   • Count how many additions you need to turn each of your numbers into a palindrome. Stop if your total is over 1000.

   • Colour the numbers on the PCM to show how many additions it takes to make each number a palindrome. Use a different colour for one addition, two additions, three additions and more than three additions.

   21 becomes a palindrome in 1 step: 21 + 12 = 33

> **Look for patterns in your coloured table. Do more numbers become palindromes after one or two additions? Which numbers go over 1000?**

Subtraction matching game

Rhys had £6·43 in his pocket. He bought some food for £1·50.

1 How much does he have left?

Look at the sets of cards from PCM 30.
Set I is the money you start with.
Set 2 is the money you spend.
Set 3 is the money you have left.

2 Match up the cards in threes to show the money you start with, the money you spend and the amount you have left. Make sure all the cards match up.
Write down your subtractions and answers as you go.

$$£6·43 - £1·59 = £4·84$$

3 Pair up the cards from Set I and Set 2 in different ways to make new totals using subtraction. Write your totals on the blank cards from PCM 30. Swap your new sets with a partner. Try matching up your partner's cards and totals.

 Make your own matching game using different types of numbers. For example, you could use larger numbers, lengths in metres and centimetres or time in hours and minutes. You can choose whether to use addition or subtraction.

Missing-number subtractions

Find the missing numbers.

1   705   −      =   399

2   ⭐   −   45   =   588

3   £9·23   −   ⭐   =   £5·77

4   ⭐   −   £4·49   =   £3·32

5   8 m 37 cm   −   ⭐   =   6 m 69 cm

6   ⭐   −   3 m 37 cm   =   4 m 75 cm

- Start with two 3-digit numbers.   **350 and 420**
- Find the difference between them.   **70**
- Subtract your two numbers from 1000.   **650 and 580**
- Find the difference between your two new numbers.   **70**

7   Investigate other pairs of 3-digit numbers.

What do you notice? Can you explain it?

eXtra

Complete these number sentences.
The two missing numbers are the same for each sentence.

⭐ + ⭐ = 504

⭐ + 136 = ⭐

The bill

Three friends have a meal at The Sunburnt Prawn restaurant in Sydney, Australia. They select from the menu on PCM 31. Each person has a starter, a main course and a dessert.

Amie always chooses seafood for her starter and her main course.
Bart is a vegetarian. He has the cheese board for dessert.
Chan wants to try lots so she has the taster plate as a starter and dessert.

This is the bill. The totals are in Australian dollars.

Starters	$113·90
Main course	$186·30
Desserts	$123·40
Total	$423·60

1 What does each person have to eat?

2 How much does each person's meal cost?

This is an accounting grid. The totals are added across and down. They should add up both ways.

	Amie	Bart	Chan	Total
Starter				
Main				
Dessert				
Total				

3 Copy and complete this accounting grid to check your answers.

The friends order hot drinks. Amie has China tea. Chan has coffee. The new bill comes to $61·90. What drink did Bart have? Make a new accounting grid to work out the final totals. How much did each friend pay in total?

Multiplying by doubling and halving

Not all people multiply numbers the way we do. People from the past and people from different cultures may do it differently. Some people use doubling and halving to do multiplication! This is sometimes called peasant multiplication.

The numbers on the left are doubled each time. The numbers on the right are halved. If there is a remainder, it is not written.

Add together all the numbers on the left that are next to an odd number on the right. This is the answer.

XV × XII	
~~XV~~	XII
~~XXX~~	VI
LX	III
CXX	I

CXX + LX = CLXXX

15 × 12	
~~15~~	12
~~30~~	6
60	3
120	1

120 + 60 = 180

> How do you think this method works?

Answer questions 1–3 on PCM 34.
Complete the multiplication charts to find the answers.
Check your answers with a calculator.

Remember to cross out the doubled numbers that you don't need.

Find the mistakes in questions 4–6 on PCM 34.

Write out the correct workings and answers in the empty charts.

eXtra

Use the peasant multiplication method to check divisions. Is 375 ÷ 25 = 15 correct? Multiply 15 by 25 using doubling and halving to check.

Maximising products

With digit cards 2, 3 and 4 and × and = you can make six products.

| 2 | 3 | × | 4 | = | | 2 | 4 | × | 3 | = |

| 3 | 2 | × | 4 | = | | 3 | 4 | × | 2 | = |

| 4 | 2 | × | 3 | = | | 4 | 3 | × | 2 | = |

1 Work out the multiplications above.
Which product is the largest?
This number is called the maximum product.

For each set of three numbers, find the maximum product.

2 2, 3 and 5   **3** 3, 4 and 5

4 3, 4 and 9   **5** 2, 8 and 9

Compare your answers with a partner.
Use a calculator to check if they are right.

Are there patterns for how the digits are placed to give the maximum products?

6 Use four digit cards to make a multiplication like this:

Find the product. What is the highest product you can make using your four digits? Compare with a partner and discuss what you notice.

 Play an estimating game. Lay out four digit cards in a row.
Place a × sign somewhere in between the cards.
For example, 3 9 × 1 5.
One of your group uses a calculator to find the product
but keeps it secret. The rest of the group estimate the
answer. The player with the nearest estimate wins.
Swap so that each player has a turn with the calculator.

Into the unknown

If you know this...   ...do you know the answers to these?

$4 \times 8 = 32$

40×8

40×80

4×80

$32 \div 8$

$320 \div 4$

$32 \div 4$

$320 \div 8$

$320 \div 40$

$320 \div 80$

I Use the two known facts on PCM 35 to finish the unknown facts.
Add any other facts you think of.

Solve these multiplications.

2 40×32 **3** 33×60 **4** 50×28

5 26×30 **6** 70×24 **7** 13×90

Write down your working to show how you solved them.

These multiplications look hard. Can you explain how you made them easier?

eXtra Add I to either of the numbers in the multiplications you did earlier. Write down the answers to your new multiplications. Is there a pattern in your new answers?
If $30 \times 26 = 780$, what number could add to 780 to find 31×26?
What about 30×27?

Sharing camels

In ancient Egypt, a father shared his camels between three children.

- He gave half of his camels to the eldest child.
- The second child got a third of his camels.
- The youngest child got a ninth of his camels.

But he had 17 camels. The children did not know how to split them! Then their aunt gave them her only camel as a gift. The children shared out the camels and the aunt got her camel back.

> Can you see how the extra camel solves the problem?

Use unit fractions to answer these questions.

> In a unit fraction the top number is 1.

1 What if the number of camels is not 17? Can they be shared? Investigate the problem with four different numbers of camels. What do you find?

2 Explore what happens if there are two children and 17 camels. What if there are four children?

3 Make up your own story like this. Finish your story by saying how to solve the problem.

> Make sure the fractions you use do not add up to 1.

> How could you extend this investigation?

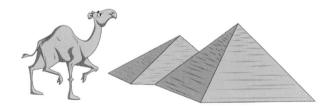

eXtra Your share of camels is $\frac{1}{2}$ and you get 12 camels. How many camels are there altogether? Explore different unit fractions and numbers of camels. Find the total number of camels each time. What patterns can you see?

Fractions in order

I Look at the kites flying above the fraction number line on PCM 36. Draw strings to tie the kites to the right places on the number line.

Kite card game

- Use the kite cards from PCM 36 and the number line on PCM 37.
- Shuffle the cards and place them face down.
- Take turns to pick a card. Place your card on a kite on the number line.
- Draw a string to join the kite to the right place on the number line. Kite strings cannot cross each other.
- If you cannot place a card on a kite, miss a go and keep the card.
- When the cards have run out or the kites are all full, the game is over. The player who has the lowest number of cards is the winner.

Ladder card game

- Use the ladder cards from PCM 36 and the ladder on PCM 37.
- Shuffle the cards and place them face down.
- Take turns to pick a card. Place your card on the ladder.
- The numbers above your card must be larger than it. The numbers below your card must be smaller than it.
- If you cannot place a card on the ladder, miss a go and keep the card.
- When the cards have run out or the ladder is full, the game is over. The player who has the lowest number of cards is the winner.

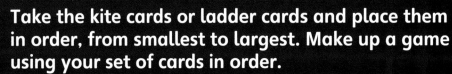

e**X**tra Take the kite cards or ladder cards and place them in order, from smallest to largest. Make up a game using your set of cards in order.

Estimating perimeters and areas

The sides of this rectangle are 10 cm by 8 cm, to the nearest centimetre.

The perimeter would be 36 cm and the area would be 80 cm^2. But the measurements are not exact.

The rectangle could be as small as 9·5 cm by 7·5 cm with a perimeter of 34 cm. The rectangle could be as large as 10·4 cm by 8·4 cm with a perimeter of 37·6 cm.

The areas of the smallest and largest possible rectangles can be worked out using grids. Copy and complete the grids below.

1

×	9	$\frac{1}{2}$
7		
$\frac{1}{2}$		$\frac{1}{4}$

2

×	10	0·4
8		3·2
0·4		0·16

> $\frac{1}{4}$ and 0·16 are quite small compared to the other products. Do you think it is important to add them to the total area?

These rectangles are measured to the nearest centimetre. Find the minimum and maximum perimeters for these rectangles. Find the minimum and maximum areas using grids.

3 6 cm by 8 cm
4 7 cm by 9 cm
5 9 cm by 11 cm
6 10 cm by 12 cm
7 11 cm by 13 cm
8 12 cm by 14 cm

Explore how exact measuring can be. Look at a square with 10 cm sides. What are the possible perimeters to the nearest cm of this square if you measure the sides to the nearest $\frac{1}{2}$ cm? What if you measure to the nearest 2 mm? Or to the nearest 1 mm?

The Gattegno chart

Caleb Gattegno (1911–1988) was famous for his ideas on teaching mathematics. He invented the Gattegno chart, which you can see on PCM 41.

Multiplying by 10 with the Gattegno chart
- Choose a number.   **365**
- Partition your number and find the hundreds, tens and units in the correct rows.   **3 hundreds, 6 tens, 5 units**
- Slide them up one row.   **30 × 100 + 60 × 10 + 50 × 1**
- Work out your new number.   **3650**

1   Complete the Gattegno chart on PCM 41.

2   Use your chart to multiply some more numbers by 10.

3   How would you use the chart to divide by 10?

4   How would you use it to multiply and divide by 100?

Look at the left-hand column of the chart.

5   Work out how to multiply and divide by all these numbers.

Gattegno knew that doubling and halving could make his chart even more useful.

6   Pick a 2-digit number. Double it in your head. Multiply it by 1000 using the chart. You have just multiplied your 2-digit number by 2000!

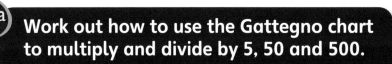

eXtra   **Work out how to use the Gattegno chart to multiply and divide by 5, 50 and 500.**

Subtraction walls

Here are two number walls.

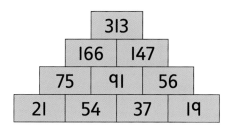

Addition

267	189	421	350
	78	232	71
		154	161
			7

Subtraction

Use the blank subtraction walls on PCM 42.

1 Put 5, 95, 125 and 225 in the top row of a wall. What is the bottom number? Try putting the top numbers in different orders. Can the bottom number ever be zero?

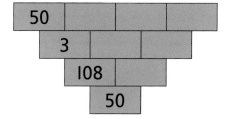

2 Try again with 29, 137, 270 and 378.

Put these numbers in order in the left bricks of a wall. Fill in the wall.

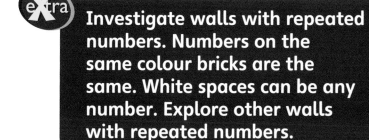

3 50, 3, 108 and 50

4 1086, 1759, 686 and 371

5 Make a symmetrical wall.

6 Make a wall where all numbers have the same amount of digits. For example, 3-digit numbers.

7 Make a wall with a fixed bottom number, for example 100.

8 Make a wall with an extra row of five bricks at the top.

eXtra Investigate walls with repeated numbers. Numbers on the same colour bricks are the same. White spaces can be any number. Explore other walls with repeated numbers.

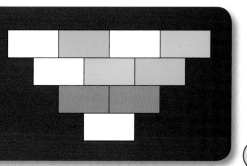

Matching subtractions

Can you make difficult subtractions easier by looking for patterns?

Here is a way of showing 216 – 148 on a number line.

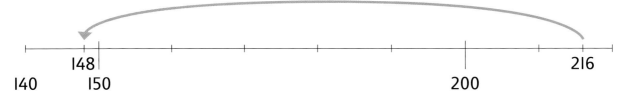

1   How far is it from 148 to 216? Is it the same for 218 – 150?
    What about 118 – 50?

Look at

405 – 187

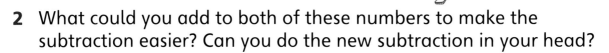

2   What could you add to both of these numbers to make the
    subtraction easier? Can you do the new subtraction in your head?

Turn these into easier subtractions, keeping the answer the same.

3   341 – 198   4   229 – 152   5   807 – 529   6   753 – 395

Use the cards from PCM 43 and find the matching subtractions.

*   Work out the subtractions.
*   Sort the cards by their answers. Is there a pattern?
*   Find the missing subtractions in the patterns.
*   Now try to extend the patterns in both directions.

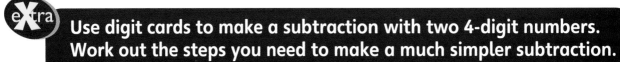

extra   **Use digit cards to make a subtraction with two 4-digit numbers.
Work out the steps you need to make a much simpler subtraction.
Do the simple subtraction in your head. For example**
            9503 – 7864 is the same as
                    2503 – 864 is the same as
                            2539 – 900 is the same as
                                    2639 – 1000

Patterns in subtractions

Can you explain the patterns you see when you subtract numbers with consecutive digits?

Here is a way of making a pattern of subtractions.

- Take three consecutive digits and make a 3-digit number.   **234**
- Reverse the digits.   **432**
- Subtract the smaller number from the larger.   **432 – 234**

1   Make up as many of these subtractions as you can. Can you see a pattern? Can you explain why it happens?

2   What happens when you use consecutive odd digits to make a pattern? How about consecutive even digits?

Here are some more patterns to explore and explain.

3   630 – 036   741 – 147   852 – 258

4   4321 – 1234   5432 – 2345   6543 – 3456

5   £5·43 – £3·21   £6·54 – £4·32   £7·65 – £5·43

6   £65·43 – £43·21   £76·54 – £54·32   £87·65 – £65·43

Take three consecutive odd or even 2-digit numbers. Join them up then reverse them to make a 6-digit subtraction pattern.
For example 12, 14 and 16 would be 614121 – 121416 = 492705.
Use a calculator to explore these subtractions.
Explain any patterns that you find.

Kaprekar's numbers

Dattatreya Ramachandra Kaprekar was born in India in 1905. As a child he spent many happy hours solving maths puzzles. This love of numbers continued throughout his life.

Kaprekar was a gifted mathematician, who discovered many new facts and developed theories to explain them. Two of the numbers he discovered are now called Kaprekar's constant and Kaprekar's number.

Kaprekar's constant: 1089

Write any 3-digit number.

Write a second 3-digit number by reversing the digits of the first number.

$$731 - 137 = 594$$
$$594 + 495 = 1089$$

Subtract the smaller number from the larger number.

Take the answer, reverse the digits and add the two new numbers.

1 Are there any starting numbers that do not give the answer 1089?

Kaprekar's number: 6174

Take any four digit cards and use them to make the largest possible 4-digit number. Write the number.

$$7631 - 1367 = 6264$$
$$6642 - 2466 = 4176$$
$$7641 - 1467 = 6174$$

Now use the same cards to make the smallest possible number. Write it down.

Subtract the smaller number from the larger number.

Is the answer 6174? If so, stop. If not, use the answer to select your next four digit cards and start again.

2 What happens if you repeat the process after you have reached 6174?

eXtra Try the process for Kaprekar's constant with 2-digit numbers. What happens? What about 4-digit numbers?

Multiplying and dividing by 9

9 is 1 less than 10.

You can use this fact to multiply any number by 9.
These grids show how this is done.

×	7
10	70
⁻1	⁻7

×	47
10	470
⁻1	⁻47

×	351
10	3510
⁻1	⁻351

$9 \times 7 = 70 - 7$
$\qquad = 63$

$9 \times 47 = 470 - 47$
$\qquad = 423$

$9 \times 351 = 3510 - 351$
$\qquad = 3159$

These grids can also help to show dividing by 9.

$9 \times 7 = 63$
So $63 \div 9 = 7$

$9 \times 47 = 423$
So $423 \div 9 = 47$

$9 \times 351 = 3159$
So $3159 \div 9 = 351$

1   Make up four of your own multiplications by 9 and show them on grids. Rewrite your multiplications to show dividing by 9.

Play the matching game using the cards in Set A on PCM 44.

2   Write down the 10 pairs of multiplications and answers.

 e**X**tra

Here are two special numbers, 1089 and 9109.

×1	1089
×2	2178
×3	

×1	9109
×2	18 218
×3	

Copy and complete the multiplication tables up to × 10. Check your results with a calculator. Describe any patterns you can see.

B3

Digital roots

To find the digital root of a number, add its digits together.

If the answer has more than one digit, add its digits together until you reach a single-digit number.

To find the digital root of 75:

Add its digits. $7 + 5 = 12$

Add the digits in the answer.
          $1 + 2 = 3$

The digital root of 75 is 3.

Does $75 \times 47 = 3525$?
Without doing the multiplication, check the digital roots.
75×47 has digital roots of 3×2, which equals 6.
If 3525 also has a digital root of 6 it may be the right answer.

Solve these multiplications, then check using digital roots.

1 25×40 **2** 23×17 **3** 44×35 **4** 98×11

Does $1014 \div 13 = 78$?
Use digital roots to check the inverse calculation: $13 \times 78 = 1014$.
$4 \times 6 = 24$. This has a digital root of 6.
1014 also has a digital root of 6, so the division is probably correct.

Solve these divisions, then check using digital roots.

5 $192 \div 8$ **6** $175 \div 7$ **7** $224 \div 16$ **8** $399 \div 21$

How does the digital root method of checking calculations work?

eXtra Look at the table on PCM 45. Check the digital roots of the numbers in the column with 5 at the top. What do you notice? Divide these numbers by 9 and check the remainders. Predict other patterns in the table. Were your predictions right?

Bearings

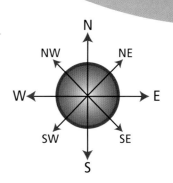

> Bearings are angles in all four directions.
> They are used in orienteering, navigation
> and on radar screens.
> Bearings start from 0° (north) and move
> clockwise, so the bearing for east is 090°.

Give the compass directions with these bearings.

I 180° **2** 270°

North-east has a bearing of 045°. Give the bearings for:

3 south-east **4** north-west **5** south-west

South-south-east is half-way between south and south-east.
Give the bearings for:

6 south-south-east **7** north-north-east **8** west-south-west

9 north-north-west **10** east-south-east **II** east-north-east

Two coastguard lookout points are 20 km apart. The line between them
runs west to east. One lookout sees a boat on a bearing of 240° and the
other sees the same boat on a bearing of 120°.

12 How far away from each lookout is the boat? Accurately draw a
diagram like this to help you. You could use 20 cm to represent 20 km.

**On a local map, find three points of interest that are quite
far apart. Find the bearings that someone at each point
would give for the other two points. Measure the straight-
line distances between the three points. What do you
notice about your results?**

Paper-folding angles

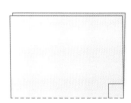

Fold a piece of paper in half width-ways.
You have made a right angle! A right angle is 90°.
Fix the right angle in place with glue or sticky tape
and mark it I. Cut out the angle.

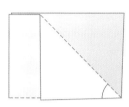

Make another right angle then fold it in half, like this.
You have made half a right angle! How many
degrees is that? Fix the angle in place with glue or
sticky tape and mark it $\frac{1}{2}$. Cut out the angle.

Make another half right angle then unfold it, like
this. You have made one and a half right angles!
How many degrees is that? Fix the angle in place with
glue or sticky tape and mark it $1\frac{1}{2}$. Cut out the angle.

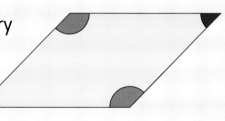

Draw around your angles to make a polygon.
The lengths of the sides do not matter, but every
inside angle must be $\frac{1}{2}$, I or $1\frac{1}{2}$ right angles.
For example, this polygon has four sides and
its angles are $\frac{1}{2}$, $1\frac{1}{2}$, $\frac{1}{2}$, and $1\frac{1}{2}$ right angles.
Its angle total is four right angles.

> Two polygons are the same if they have the same number
> of sides, and the same angles in the same order.

I How many different polygons can you make using these angles?
   Is there a pattern?

2 Find the angle total for each polygon. Is there a relationship between
   the number of sides a polygon has and its angle total?

eXtra **Use PCM 46 to make $\frac{1}{3}$, $\frac{2}{3}$ $1\frac{1}{3}$ and $1\frac{2}{3}$ of a right angle.
What new polygons can you make using these new
angles and your other angles? What do you notice
about the angle totals of your new polygons?**

Roads between towns

Three new towns

There are two competing plans for the system of roads connecting the new towns Ayton, Beeton and Ceeton.

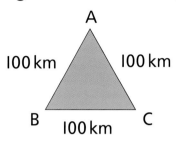

Plan A places the towns 100 km apart at the corners of an equilateral triangle. This is 300 km of roads.

Plan B places the towns at the corners of a square with sides of 100 km. The fourth corner of the square is empty. This is about 340 km of roads.

I Investigate other road systems for each plan. What is the shortest possible road system for each plan? Roads do not need to run along the edges of the triangles.

Four new towns

Ayton, Beeton, Ceeton and Deeton are to be built using Plan C. The four towns are at the corners of a square with sides of 100 km. Connecting the towns with a simple square of roads would mean a road system totalling 400 km.

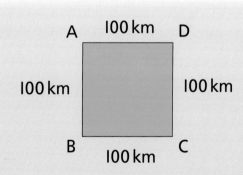

2 Investigate other ways of joining the four towns with four roads. What is the shortest possible road system?

In Plan D, the four towns are at the corners of a rhombus. The sides are 100 km, but the angles are not right angles. What is the shortest possible road system? How does it compare to your solution for Plan C?

63

Mass and weight

Mass measures how much matter an object contains.
It is measured in kilograms (kg).
An object's mass stays the same wherever it is.

Weight measures how much an object is being pulled by gravity.
It is measured in newtons (N).
An object's weight changes if the force of gravity acting on it changes.

In other parts of our Solar System the force of gravity is not the same as it is here on Earth.

Solar System body	Gravity
Earth's Moon	about $\frac{1}{6}$ of Earth's
The planet Mars	about $\frac{3}{8}$ of Earth's
Saturn's moon, Titan	about $\frac{1}{10}$ of Earth's

Titan

On Earth an object with a mass of 1 kilogram weighs about 10 newtons.

How much would you weigh on Titan? Let's say you have a mass of 35 kg. This means you weigh 350 newtons on Earth. Titan's gravity is about $\frac{1}{10}$ of Earth's gravity, so you would weigh about 35 newtons on Titan.

1 Copy and complete this table.

Object	Mass (kg)	Approximate weight (N) on:			
		Earth	Mars	Moon	Titan
A child	30	300			
A bicycle	15	150			
A family car	1250	12 500			
A lorry	2 000	20 000			
Eiffel Tower	8 million	80 million			

2 Find out the masses of five other items and add them to the table.

eXtra   **Find out about gravity on other planets and moons in the Solar System. Draw a new table to compare weights.**

Half times

A family travels by car to their holiday destinations. They decide to stop for a 10 minute break half-way through each journey.

1 For each journey at what time should the family take a break? Copy and complete the table.

> Don't forget to think about how long their breaks are.

	Start time	Half-time break	Predicted arrival time
1	9 am		12:44 pm
2	10:15 am		3:31 pm
3	11:30 am		2:08 pm
4	12:45 pm		7:05 pm

2 Copy and complete this table, to the nearest minute, with the journeys from question 1.

	Start time	Journey duration	Time when fraction of journey left			
			Half	Third	Quarter	Tenth
1	9 am					
2	10:15 am					
3	11:30 am					
4	12:45 pm					

If people work on bank holidays, they are paid more. If they are paid $1\frac{1}{2}$ times their usual hourly rate, this is called 'time and a half'. Other rates are 'time and a quarter' and 'double time'. Make up some word problems with time and a half, time and a quarter and double time.

Carroll and Venn diagrams

Lewis Carroll

Lewis Carroll was the pen name used by Charles Dodgson (1832–1898). He is best known for his book *Alice's Adventures in Wonderland*. He invented the logic diagrams now known as Carroll diagrams.

John Venn

John Venn (1834–1923) invented what we now call Venn diagrams. These use a background rectangle containing the set of all the things being considered. Inside this are one, two or three circles. Each circle contains the members of the set that have a particular property.

What information do these Carroll and Venn diagrams show?

	Less than 10	10 or more
Odd number	1 3 5 7 9	11 13 15 17 19
Even number	2 4 6 8	10 12 14 16 18 20

Carroll diagram

2   1   11   10   14   6
3   13   15   12   16
5
7   17   18
4   9   19   20   8

Odd numbers   10 or more

Venn diagram

Make a Carroll diagram and a Venn diagram to answer the pairs of questions. Put at least two numbers or shapes in each zone.

1 2-digit numbers: *Is it a multiple of five?*
                          Is its digital root an even number?

2 Quadrilaterals: *Has it got two lines of symmetry?*
                          Has it got a pair of parallel sides?

e**X**tra   **Can you draw a Venn diagram that answers three questions? Make up some sorting problems using your diagram and ask a friend to solve them.**

Putting data into logic diagrams

1 Choose **either** numbers **or** shapes.
Choose any **two** questions from the list.
Draw **either** a Venn **or** a Carroll diagram for your questions.
Place **10** of the listed numbers or shapes into your diagram.

Number questions	Shape questions
• Is it even? • Is it a multiple of 5? • Is it a square number? • Is its digital root a multiple of 3?	• Is it a quadrilateral? • Does it have a right angle? • Does it have at least two lines of symmetry? • Does it have at least one pair of parallel sides? • Does it have only two different angle sizes?

A square number is made by multiplying a whole number by itself. 16 is a square number. It is 4 times 4.

NUMBERS

75	77	81	84
88	90	96	99
100	101	104	105
108	111	120	121

SHAPES

2 Make three more diagrams, to end up with two Venn and two Carroll diagrams. Make two diagrams with numbers and two diagrams with shapes.

eX**tra** Do you prefer Venn diagrams or Carroll diagrams? Why?
Does it matter whether you are sorting shapes or numbers?

Back numbers

Amir, Becky and Chris each have a number on their backs. They cannot see their own number. They give these clues about the numbers they can see on the other children's backs.

I can see two numbers that add to 100.

The numbers on Amir and Chris add to 120.

I can see a total of 80.

1 Work out the number on each child's back.

2 If the numbers were 87, 99 and 105, what three totals would the children give?

3 Think of another set of three numbers. What are the totals? Is there a pattern?

4 Play this game in threes. Each choose a number and place it on someone's back. Add the numbers you can see, and tell the group your total. Each work out the number on your own back.

Amir, Becky and Chris play the game twice more, then play with Dhara. Work out the amount on each child's back from their totals.

5 Amir: 82   Becky: 111   Chris: 99

6 Amir: £11·50   Becky: £12·70   Chris: £12·60

7 Amir: £85   Becky: £99   Chris: £97   Dhara: £103

8 Amir: 1500   Becky: 1453   Chris: 1589   Dhara: 1674

---

eXtra Explore other ways to report the numbers you can see. If there are two numbers you could multiply them, or subtract one from the other. Does that make the activity easier or more difficult?

Subtraction options

This is a spider diagram. A subtraction goes inside the body. A different way of doing the calculation goes at the end of each leg.

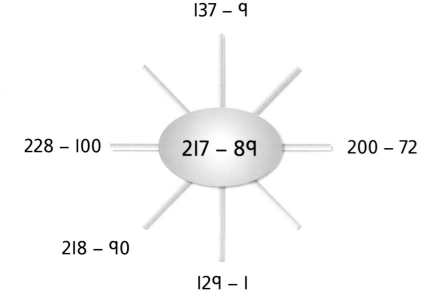

137 − 9

228 − 100   217 − 89   200 − 72

218 − 90

129 − 1

Can you see how the subtraction has been changed each time?

Which leg do you find easiest to calculate?

Draw a spider diagram for each of these subtractions.
Fill in as many legs as you can.

1   320 − 185   2   £9·30 − £4·80

3   1415 − 980   4   £31·20 − £7·95

5   562 − 499   6   £8·82 − £2·89

7   £16·44 − £7·54   8   £45·12 − £18·34

9   £72·09 − £28·51   10 £140·45 − £82·69

Don't forget to check your answers.
You could use addition or digital roots.

 Use digit cards to make some subtractions with money values in pounds and pence. Find several options for each subtraction, and choose the easiest option for your calculation.

Half-price sale

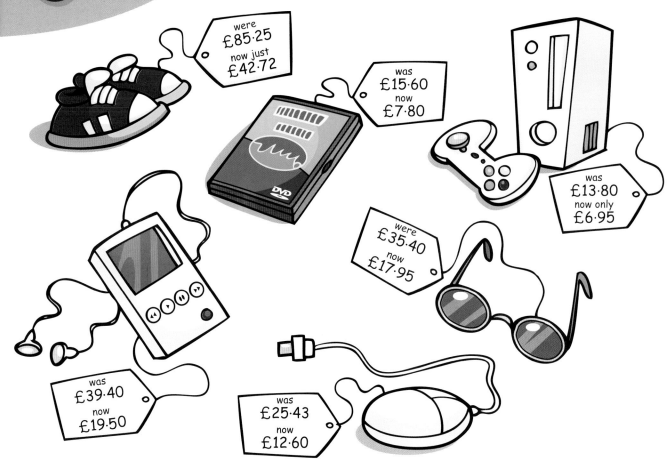

These items are in an up-to-half-price sale.

> Which items are exactly half price?
> Which items cost a little more than half price?
> Which items cost a little less than half price?

Answer the questions on PCM 48.

eXtra

Here are the prices of some other sale items.

£15   £24   £10   £8   £30

This time you only know the sale price. Work out the original price of each item if the sale price is:
- half price
- $\frac{1}{3}$ off
- $\frac{1}{4}$ off
- 10% off

John Napier (1550–1617) was a very inventive mathematician. He invented logarithms, to make calculations quicker and easier. Other mathematicians used Napier's logarithms in a new calculation device called a slide rule.

By sliding one strip along the other you can read the results of multiplications and divisions!

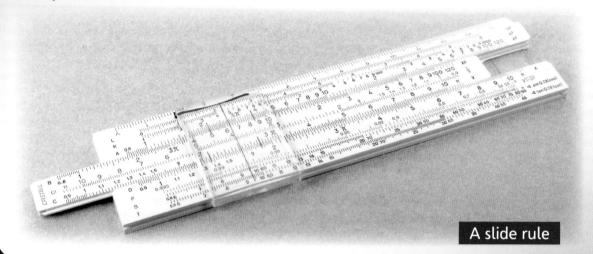

A slide rule

I What do you notice about how the numbers on the slide rule scale are placed? Are there any patterns?

Look at the nomogram on PCM 49. To multiply, draw a straight line from a number on the top scale to a number on the bottom scale. Read the product where the straight line crosses the middle scale.

Answer these multiplications using the nomogram.

2 $2 \times 8 =$ **3** $2 \cdot 5 \times 10 =$ **4** $4 \times 9 =$ **5** $3 \times 6 =$

Try these divisions using the nomogram.

6 $72 \div 8 =$ **7** $56 \div 7 =$ **8** $48 \div 6 =$ **9** $63 \div 9 =$

The numbers on a slide rule only go up to 100. How could you use a slide rule to calculate with larger numbers, such as 3-digit or 4-digit numbers?

Investigating patterns from 7s

Units pattern in the 7 times-table

1 Write out the 7 times-table.

2 Copy out the pattern of the units digits. Continue the pattern.

3 Which other times-tables have units digit patterns that include all 10 digits?

> Which pattern is the ×1 pattern backwards?

How many 7s?

4 How many 7s are there in:

   10   100   1000   10 000   100 000   1 000 000   10 000 000

5 Write the units digit pattern of your answers in a circle, with arrows between the digits.

Looking at sevenths

$\frac{1}{7}$ 1 ÷ 7 =

$\frac{2}{7}$ 2 ÷ 7 =

$\frac{3}{7}$ 3 ÷ 7 =

0.142857142857

6 Use a calculator to complete this pattern up to $\frac{7}{7}$.

7 How does this pattern link to the pattern in question 5?

8 Explore larger numbers such as $\frac{10}{7}$ and $\frac{39}{7}$.

e**X**tra

A cube number is a number multiplied by itself and multiplied by itself again.

Use a calculator to explore the link between cube numbers and multiples of 7.

For example:

2 × 2 × 2 = 8 is one more than 1 × 7 = 7.

3 × 3 × 3 = 27 is one less than 4 × 7 = 28.

Find a cube number that is not next door to a multiple of 7.

Factor record-breakers

Here are factor tables for 14, 21 and 28.

14	
1	14
2	7

Factors are
1, 2, 7, 14

21	
1	21
3	7

Factors are
1, 3, 7, 21

28	
1	28
2	14
4	7

Factors are
1, 2, 4, 7, 14, 28

1 Draw factor tables for the numbers 1 to 15.

A factor record-breaker is the first number with a new number of factors.
1 is a record-breaker because it is the first number with one factor.
2 is a record-breaker because it is the first number with two factors.

2 Copy and continue this table to find the factor record-breakers for numbers up to 100.

Record-breaker	Factors	Number of factors
1	1	1
2	1, 2	2
4	1, 2, 4	3
6		

3 Circle the record-breakers on PCM 51.

4 Colour the numbers which have the same number of factors.
Use a different colour for each number of factors.

Can you see any patterns in the numbers of factors?

 What is the first factor record-breaker after 100?
Use a calculator to find more record-breakers.
How far can you get?

E3

Multiplication patterns

How can you use patterns to solve multiplications without multiplying?

Copy these multiplications and find the products. Continue the patterns as long as you can. Check your answers with a calculator.

1

9 × 12	= 108
9 × 23	= 207
9 × 34	=

Carry this on to 9 × 89.

2

9 × 123	= 1107
9 × 234	= 2106
9 × 345	=
9 × 456	=

3

9 × 11	= 99
19 × 21	=
29 × 31	=

4

20 × 20	= 400
19 × 21	=
18 × 22	=

5 How many rows do the patterns last for? What happens when the patterns end?

6 Continue this pattern up to 10 × 1089. What do you notice?

1 × 1089	= 1089
2 × 1089	= 2178
3 × 1089	=

7 Continue this pattern up to 10 × 9109. What do you notice?

1 × 9109	= 9109
2 × 9109	= 18 218
3 × 9109	=

eXtra

50 × 50 = 2500. This is called 50 squared or 50^2. Carry on a pattern with 51 × 51, 52 × 52. What do you notice? How long does the pattern last for?

Napier's bones

John Napier invented a multiplying tool called Napier's bones.

Each bone contains a times table. The tens digit is above the diagonal line and the units digit is below the line. The bones are placed next to each other to make a number. The index bone is the number you are multiplying by.

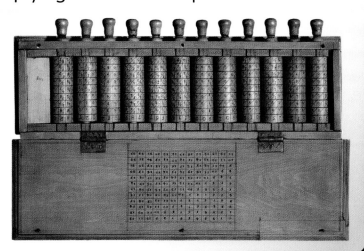

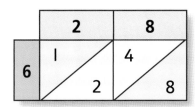

Here is 6 × 28.
Remember that the left bone shows 6 × 20, not 6 × 2.
The 1 is 100. The 2 is 20. The 4 is 40.
6 × 28 = 100 + 20 + 40 + 8 = 168

Try these multiplications using Napier's bones from PCM 52.

1 4 × 23   **2** 5 × 36   **3** 6 × 47

4 7 × 25   **5** 8 × 57   **6** 9 × 46

7 Use three bones to multiply 8 × 152.

8 Use Napier's bones to work out the 215 times table up to 9 × 215.

Can you use the bones to multiply two 2-digit numbers?
Can the bones be used to do division?

At the time of Elizabeth the First, people used gelosia multiplication. Use the internet to find out how gelosia multiplication works. Make up some multiplications and work them out using gelosia multiplication.

Fractions of a square

Look at these tile patterns.

Lines cross.	Lines meet.	Lines do not meet.
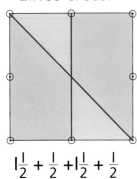	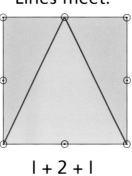	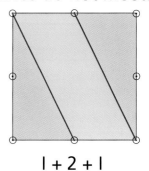
$1\frac{1}{2} + \frac{1}{2} + 1\frac{1}{2} + \frac{1}{2}$	$1 + 2 + 1$	$1 + 2 + 1$

I   Use the blank squares on PCM 53 to make some tiles.
To make a tile draw two straight lines between
any dots on the square.

> What different lengths could your lines be?

2   How many different tiles can you make?

> Are all your pieces different?
> Are they still different if you turn
> them around or turn them over?

> What symmetry do
> your tiles have?

Each tile can be made into four small squares.
In the first tile the shapes are $1\frac{1}{2} + \frac{1}{2} + 1\frac{1}{2} + \frac{1}{2}$ squares.

The triangle in the first tile is $\frac{1}{2}$ a small square.

The quadrilateral shape is $1\frac{1}{2}$ small squares.

3   Investigate the fractions and mixed numbers in your tiles.

 eXtra   **Make up a game using the shapes on your tiles and
their fractions. Play your game with a partner.**

Missing fractions and decimals

Solve these missing-number problems.

1 $\dfrac{1}{2}$ of 3 4 = ⬚ ⬚

2 $\dfrac{2}{5}$ of 4 0 = ⬚ ⬚

3 Use digit cards 0–9 to make new problems like these. Work out the missing numbers in your new problems.

Here are the answers to some fraction problems. Find the questions.

| There may be more than one question. |

4 18   **5** 30   **6** 54   **7** 42

Solve these missing-number problems.

8 1 4 · 5 + 2 · 3 = ⬚ ⬚ · ⬚

9 7 2 · 9 + 4 · 6 = ⬚ ⬚ · ⬚

10 Use digit cards 0–9 to make some more problems like these. Use each digit card only once. Work out the answers.

 Are these fractions and decimals equal?

$\dfrac{1}{2}$ = 0 · 5 $\dfrac{3}{5}$ = 0 · 6

Make up some more pairs of decimals and fractions using digit cards. How many equal pairs can you find?

Author team
Adrian Pinel
Jeni Pinel

Part of Pearson

Ginn is an imprint of Pearson Education Limited, a company incorporated in England and Wales, having its registered office at Edinburgh Gate, Harlow, Essex, CM20 2JE. Registered company number: 872828

www.pearsonschools.co.uk

Ginn is a registered trademark of Pearson Education Limited

Text © Pearson Education Limited 2009

First published 2009

13 12 11 10
10 9 8 7 6 5 4 3

British Library Cataloguing in Publication Data
A catalogue record for this book is available from the British Library

ISBN 978 0 602 57774 2

Typeset by Artistix
Original illustrations © Pearson Education Limited 2009
Illustrated by Matt Buckley, Andy Hammond, John Haslam, Andrew Painter, Anthony Rule and Q2A
Cover photo/illustration © Per José Karlén
Printed in China (CTPS/03)

Acknowledgements
The authors and publisher would like to thank the following individuals and organisations for permission to reproduce photographs:
© Shutterstock / Victor Burnside, Clock face, p4; © Ancient Art & Architecture / Ronald Sheridan, Counting board, p4; © Shutterstock / Slowfish, Sloth bear, p16; © Shutterstock / Mateusz Drozd, Brown bear, p16; © Digital Vision, Giant panda, p16; © Digital Vision, Polar bear, p16; © Nature Picture Library / Eric Baccega, American black bear, p16; © Alamy Images / Arco Images GmbH, Sun bear, p16; © Photolibrary / Animals Animals, Asiatic black bear, p16; © Photolibrary / Age Fotostock, Spectacled bear, p16; © Shutterstock / Galushko Sergey, Stopwatch, p21; © Getty Images / PhotoDisc, Earth, p22; © Shutterstock / John R Smith, Thermometer, p39; © NASA - JPL - Space Science Institute, Titan, p64; © Photoshot / World Illustrated, Lewis Carroll, p66; © Getty Images / Time & Life Pictures, John Venn, p66; © Science Photo Library / Friedrich Saurer, Slide rule, p71; © Science Photo Library / Science Source, Napier's bones, p75.

Every effort has been made to contact copyright holders of material reproduced in this book. Any omissions will be rectified in subsequent printings if notice is given to the publishers.